SMALL CASTLES AND PAVILIONS OF EUROPE

SMALL CASTLES AND PAVILIONS OF EUROPE

JEROME ZERBE

INTRODUCTION BY CYRIL CONNOLLY

WALKER AND COMPANY • NEW YORK

For Margot and Roy

ACKNOWLEDGMENTS

I wish to thank the following for their help in making this book
possible: Gérald Van der Kemp, Curator of the palace of Versailles; Wilson
Randolph Gathings, my Editor at Walker and Company; and all the
people who allowed me
to photograph their homes.

JEROME ZERBE

First published in the United States of America in 1976 by the Walker Publishing Company, Inc.
Published simultaneously in Canada by Fitzhenry & Whiteside, Limited, Toronto.
ISBN: 0-8027-0542-1
Library of Congress Catalog Card Number: 76-16312
Printed in the United States of America.
10 9 8 7 6 5 4 3 2 1

CONTENTS

107
FRANCE

147
SPAIN

INTRODUCTION
by Cyril Connolly

When Jerome Zerbe and I produced *Les Pavillons*, it was in close collaboration: we confined ourselves to Paris and the Île-de-France and never ranged farther than Fontainebleau; together or separately we visited most of these architectural gems and each contributed research. Now he has outstripped me, leaving me textually as well as visually far behind. Not being blockaded behind the British currency curtain, he is free to roam at will and has brought back photographs from Russia, Sweden, Denmark, and Spain. Only in England, Italy, and Germany can I hold my own. And he, too, has been overwhelmed by the wealth at his disposal and has been forced to make a selection. Our definition of a *pavilion* is a small ornamental house where one can sleep (though not live) all the year round, where one can watch the hunt or go fishing or enjoy the "vie du château" in miniature. Even with this restriction, there remain far too many small buildings for one book. One has only to think of a city like Montpelier, with suburbs full of such small perfect buildings stretching out to the Garrigue, or of Aix and Bordeaux, Toulouse, Nancy, or the clusters along the Brenta or Vicenza or even the riot of pavilions at Stowe. And what of Hungary, Czechoslovakia, and Poland? Or the pavilions such as the Zwinger and Sanssouci, destroyed and re-erected at Dresden and Berlin? And yet some countries are singularly lacking in them—for example, Spain. One can only say that they are contrary to the temper of the Spanish people, especially the aristocracy, who lack perfections in and lightness of touch. Mr. Zerbe includes two at the Escorial, one at El Prado, and might have taken the Casa del Labrador at Aranjuez. The

1

archetype of Spanish pavilions are the Generalife and the
tower-palaces of the Alhambra, all far too well known.
Portugal he has not included, although it does possess a few examples;
one is the eighteenth-century fishing pavilion of the Marquis
de Pombal at Deiyas outside Lisbon by Mardel; another is the
beautifully detailed Quinta of the Cadavals at Cintra.

I shall never forget the day I saw it. Sunday, 14 March 1966. I had
been invited to lunch by Bertie Landsberg, the owner (since
1924) of the Villa "Malcontenta," which figures in this volume.
Finding Venice in winter bad for his health, for the last ten
years he had rented another house from the Cadavals, the Quinta de
Capiola, which he was doing up. I took the bus up to Cintra
and walked through its leafy avenues, which are lined by some of the
finest trees in Europe. Mr. and Mrs. Landsberg welcomed
me, and we had a gay lunch in the freemasonry of pavilion lovers. I
inscribed a copy of *Les Pavillons* for him, and he showed me
Arturo Lopez's privately printed book on his own pavilion at Neuilly
sent him by its previous owner, his friend Jean Rodocanachi;
the book had come out just before Mr. Lopez's death. He asked me to
look for a house with some architecture in England for the
summer. After luncheon their great friend arrived from England
(Claud Phillimore, himself an architect), and I noticed that
when introducing me, Bertie Landsberg forgot my name. Before
retiring to rest he sent us both off to see the Quinta, which
is in the purest rococo; the owners were absent. Both house and
garden were enchanting, and next door there was a stone garden
staircase with reversed herms all the way up, so that we saw one set
of heads as we went up and another coming down.

We came back and talked with Mrs. Landsberg (her husband was still
taking his siesta) and went out to the Seteais Hotel for tea.
The hotel is in one of the most beautiful buildings in Europe but was
crowded with coach parties that Sunday afternoon like a
conference at Blackpool, so we separated early and I took the bus
down through the thick mist. I was seized on the way with
uncontrollable depression, triggered off by the hordes in the hotel.
Meanwhile, my host had emerged from his siesta and

entertained a Scandinavian couple to tea. Shortly afterwards he
dropped dead. He was seventy-five. The day we had next planned to
meet him and see another quinta was the day of his funeral. The
service was held in the English church where Fielding is
buried, with several kings and ambassadors in attendance. The coffin
brushed my coat as it travelled down the aisle. On such
occasions, when the destroying angel passes so close, when the arbiter
of emptiness waves his wand and man's private universe
vanishes, one searches for signs and portents. I went over our last
conversation, about his enjoyment of Portugal for its climate,
its international society, and how it reminded him of Brazil, where he
spent his childhood. I remembered that he had been
reputedly the best-looking young man in Europe, the Cambridge
friend of Ronald Firbank, whose letters to him he had
conscientiously burnt; how he had pinched and scraped to preserve La
Malcontenta, which he had found a decaying farm whose
previous owners had removed layers of fresco and sold them, and what
he had left is one of the glories of Palladio's architecture. "I
have had a happy life," he told me as I was leaving, "I have done
everything I wanted, made love to everyone I wanted, I
have never had a moment of regret or remorse." I was reminded of
the eighteenth-century epitaph:

> Ci-gît dans une paix profondo
> Cette dame de volupté
> Qui pour plus grande sûreté
> Fit son paradis en ce monde.

But that kind of courage is no longer permissible. Like
Norman Douglas and other old men of that generation, or his younger
friend Sir Osbert Sitwell, he left one feeling that he
possessed some secret yet contagious happiness, the aesthetic's reward
for a lifetime of self-devotion—or was it that, as was written
of Arturo Lopez: "no one could meet him without wishing to become
his friend"?

It would be interesting to tabulate a character sketch of pavilion
owners down the ages to see what traits, if any, they had in
common, from the Roi Rêné to Lord Berners. Many were grand
seigneurs, royal younger sons, even reigning monarchs;

3

others were courtesans or successful businessmen or miserly eccentrics like Lord Hertford. They share an unnamed aesthetic quality which one might designate "microphily," the love of smallness—small that is, by comparison with Versailles, Blenheim, Schönbrunn—and the general standards of their time, and granted this smallness, the *l'échelle humaine* of the undertaking, it must be as perfect as possible, a bagatelle, a lüstchloss, "parva sed apta domus." They love luxury, but on such a small scale that they could sometimes afford it. One of Arturo Lopez's last actions was to order a set of silver furniture to be made for him by the only craftsman who could imitate Louis XIV. His favorite expression was "C'est très intelligent." All owners of beautiful buildings become owned by them, either because of the financial drain or because of the necessity of showing them off, of eventually being only able to see them when they were showing them off, or of handing them on intact to an heir. What is Horace Walpole without Strawberry Hill or Harold and Vita Nicolson without Sissinghurst? And yet, Europe, continent of tradition, archivism, pedigree, and the hereditary principle, is the only one to have rained bombs down on its treasures, on the Assembly Rooms at Bath, the Zwinger at Dresden, and the castles of Potsdam.

One distinct pattern emerges, however, the conjunction of patron and architect in favourable circumstances such as arose in the eighteenth century as baroque was merging into rococo. The patron should preferably be royal or a wielder of some political power, the architect a man of genius who appreciates the instinct for display. It is a short step from pavilion to bungalow once parsimony or mediocrity enter in. Moreover, posterity is unkind to these small paragons. How many times has one not come across them fallen into disrepair or used for the wrong purposes, even when the parent châteaux palaces are maintained. Maecena's villa is engulfed by suburbs, then sold, re-sold and de-forested and perhaps ends up as a garage or potato store, like Riverstown, the Bishop of Cork's stuccoed folly, near Cork. Only pavilions which form part of the ensemble of royal palaces seem certain of preservation—Bagatelle, the Trianons, the Amalienburg, for example.

4

A happy but not very well-known collaboration between
patron and architect took place in St. Petersburg (Leningrad) in the
persons of Catherine the Great and her Scottish architect,
Charles Cameron.

Cameron (1740–1812) first came to the attention of the
Empress through his published work, *The Baths of the Romans* (1772).
She had him invited by Grimm, her minister of fine art, to
whom she was writing by 1779:

> A present je me suis emparée de Mister Cameron . . . nous
> façonnons avec lui ici un jardin en terrasse avec bains en
> dessous, galerie en dessus; cela sera de beau, beau, comme dit
> Maître Blaise. . . .

She summed up the passion in a phrase which all builders
should remember:

> La fureur de bâtir est chose diabolique, cela dévore de l'argent et
> plus bâtit, plus on vent bâtir, c'est une maladie comme
> l'ivrognerie.

A sentiment with which the Prince Bishop of Würzburg,
who called it "the building bug," would have approved.

This was the celebrated Agate Pavilion.

Cameron may have been a member of the family of Cameron of
Lochiel and have been educated in Rome at the court of the
Young Pretender. The Empress thought he had Jacobite
leanings—"écossais de nation, Jacobite de profession, grand
dessinateur, nourri d'antiquités, connu par un livre
sur les bains romains."

After Catherine's death twenty years later (1796), he seems to have
lost favour and have been turned out of his house at
Tsarskoe Selo, which was, with Pavlovsk, the great palace he built for
the Grand Duke Paul, the centre of his activity. His last
years were clouded by poverty, envy, and intrigues, and before his
death he had to sell part of his library, the rest of which
went in 1812. His chief influences had been Andrea Palladio, Richard

Boyle Burlington, Robert Adam, and his draughtsman, Charles-Louis Clérisseau, who had himself worked in Russia—"cette tête fermentive est grand admirateur de Clérisseau," wrote Catherine to Grimm in 1781. He experimented in polychrome materials, using Wedgwood plaques, columns of violet glass, and the success of these new rooms was immediate. The royal apartments were followed by the Agate Pavilion, 1782–85, with its semicircular Ionic approach gallery—part Graecian, part Italian. The hot and cold baths were on the ground floor, the Agate and Jasper rooms and four smaller rooms on the first floor. John Flaxman helped with the decoration. The Cameron gallery was erected in 1783–85 and contained bronze busts of the philosophers of antiquity with the addition of one contemporary statesman, Charles James Fox, whom the Empress considered had prevented a war against Russia. He also designed the English garden. "I love to distraction these gardens in the English style—their curving lines, the gentle slopes, the ponds like lakes. My Anglomania predominates over my plutomania," she wrote to Voltaire. In the Park of Pavlovsk, the home of Paul, the heir apparent, he built a temple of friendship, the first building in Russia of the true Doric order. There were several other small buildings. His Graecian Hall in the palace of Pavlovsk was influenced by Adam's hall at Kedleston. He also renovated an old palace for Catherine in the Ukraine. As Mr. Georges Loukomski, from whom my information is derived, sums up: "Catherine alone, great Patron of Art and great Empress, was able to appreciate this poor, lonely, yet delighted Cameron. His life and work have not been easy, but he erected a monument to himself, the only building ever to have been named after its architect, one of his many masterpieces, the Kameronova Gallereia, at Tsarkoe." One wonders how he got on with Diderot, the French philosopher drawn into a dialogue of Talking Heads by the intellectual despot. The Empress, who, beginning as an obscure German princess of Anhalt-Zerbst, became more Russian than all the Russians, deposed her own husband and reigned for thirty-three years.

An even more extraordinary partnership was formed between Maximilian of Bavaria and his court dwarf, François Cuvilliés,

6

who was under four feet high. One is tempted to link his
size with the perfection of his small buildings, but he was also
responsible for the superb royal apartments in the Residenz
of Munich and for the exquisite theatre, now so happily restored.
With his masterpiece, the Amalienburg in the grounds of
the Nymphenburg Palace, he ranks immediately among the great,
great architects of the eighteenth century. It was in 1937
that I visited these gardens and came for the first time under the
pavilion's spell, as did my three companions, all younger
than I, though long since dead. The extension is unpretentious in
typical Trianon style and gives nothing away, so that the
beauty of its three main apartments is all the more overpowering. One
cannot believe it possible that rooms with their four walls,
doors and windows, could be transformed into such dream-like
evanescence of texture whose colours combine their
separate harmonies into one Mozartian whole and can be seen in
their original freshness today.

François Cuvilliés was born at Soigne-en-Hainut in 1695 (ten years
after Watteau). He was thirteen when he was appointed
court dwarf by the Elector Max Emanuel, who returned to Munich
from his exile in Paris (where he had occupied the Château
de Béarn at Saint-Cloud and run up a mountain of debts) in 1715. His
building spree up to his death in 1726 cost his Bavarian
subjects eight million florins. It was his idea for the Pagodenburg,
with its Chinese interior, which Joseph Effner carried out in
1716–19, the first breath of the rococo in Germany. Then followed the
Badenburg, also by Effner, with a bath twenty-nine by
twenty feet surmounted by a gallery. The stucco work was by
Zimmermann. It was not Max Emanuel, who died in 1726,
who gave Cuvilliés his chance but his successor, Karl Albrecht
(1726–43). Effner was allowed to decorate four of the "rich
rooms" in the Munich Residenz. Then he was dismissed, and his job
given to the young dwarf. The rococo was now in full flower,
and Cuvilliés also was employed by Karl Albrecht's brother, the
Elector of Cologne, on his palace at Bruhl as well as the next
batch of "Reichen Zimmer" at the Residenz. Zimmermann also
worked here with him.
These rooms were restored in 1963.

The Amalienburg was built in 1734–39 for the Electress Maria Amalia.
It consists of a central circular salon with two smaller rooms
on each side. The colour harmony is an alternation of blues and silver
and yellows with silver for the decoration. It is hard to say
which colour silver goes best with it. I slightly prefer the yellow. The
dome served as a platform to shoot pheasants from—only
golden and silver pheasants one feels should be permitted. He built
the Residenz theatre next in 1751–53.

Cuvilliés was consistently underestimated in France, and he certainly
owes much to the designs of Meissonier and Lajoue, yet his
own book of designs, on which he was still working at his death in
1768, proves his originality. The circular salon of the
Amalienburg was in three shades of blue on an off-white ground, with
the stucco overlaid with silver foil. The electress's bedroom
was *couleur de citron* and the hunting room *couleur de paille*.
Research has revealed the original colouring hidden under
coats of paint and proves the original scheme to have been
considerably paler. To the rear are a hall and gun-room and
kennels for the dogs. On the other side is a kitchen decorated with
blue-and-white Delft tiles. Zimmermann was the stuccoist.
"The pale blue and silver of the central salon reflected and multipled
in the mirrors contrast with the lemon and straw colour of
the rooms on either side running into the white picked out with china
blue of the outer rooms . . . once it has been seen the whole
intention of the rococo becomes lucid and self-evident" (Powell). It has
been called the most beautiful room of the eighteenth century.

The most harmonious of all these partnerships was between
Karl von Schönborn, Prince Bishop of Würzburg, and the ex-artillery
officer, Johann Balthazar Neumann, a serene and superb
architect. But their designs were too grand for this volume. Frederick
the Great and the aristocratic G. W. von Knobelsdorff had a
stormier relationship yet created the Schloss Sanssouci between them
(1745–53). The rooms where Voltaire lived and the King
died are as they left them—"I love building and decorating but only
with my own savings. Potsdam, that's what I need to be
happy" (Frederick to D'Alembert).

Next door to the Amalienburg was a glass-house, where sixteen thousand spring flowers were forced for the gardens of the pavilion. Unless it were sunk deep in the forest, the pavilion as "maison de plaisance" required gardens almost as expensive and elaborate as its interior. Vietshocheim, outside Würzburg, is an example of the rococo garden in all its perfection; another still exists at Schwitzingen, near Heidelberg, created for the Elector Palatine Carl Theodor, who became Elector of Bavaria in 1778. It contains a miniature theatre by Nicolas de Pigage, the court architect from Lunéville. On a nearby tank, surrounded by a trellised walk, bronze birds perch and spray an owl sitting in the water.

Pigage's most important building is Schloss Benrath, at Düsseldorf, which he built for Carl Theodor from 1755 to 1757. It appears to be much smaller than it is. "It is a last gesture of the rococo and on the fringe of a new age" (Powell) and is not unlike Sansouci but placed on a plinth, which Frederick the Great refused to allow von Knobelsdorff to do. Schloss Solitude, built above Stuttgart forty years later from 1763 to 1767 by J. F. Welghing and Philippe de la Guepière, according to Powell, "consists of one story raised on an arcaded gallery, with two wings extending from a small-domed pavilion. The oval windows in the central hall, the medallions over the doors, and the relative solemnity of the Doric order clearly indicate that it is already a modern building."

One cannot leave Bavaria without a thought for the late Henry (Chips) Channon—not only because of his book on the Ludwigs, which describes the many palaces of the mad King, including the one illustrated here, but also because he was the last victim of the Amalienburg and spent nearly seven thousand pounds on reproducing the main room as his dining room and employing Bavarian workmen under M. Boudini. Whatever one may think of some of his guests, one must admire his obsession. "It will be a symphony in blue and silver . . . cascades of aquamarine. Will it be London's loveliest room or is my flame dead? [1934]" There is an illustration of it in his diaries.

9

What are the chances of a poor man owning a pavilion? Very slight. Not only because of the cost but also because the moment one is empty the authorities wish to pull it down or institutionalise it. Once or twice I have come near to it myself, and I can only say that to lose one after possession is in sight, is to receive a wound that may last many years; it is like losing a fiancée. It has happened to me on more than one occasion. In Ireland there is a house called Kilshannig—the very name is like a dirge—off the road from Fermoy to Cork with four rooms with stuccoed ceilings in the style of Poussin, a columned hall and a domed staircase, the date about 1753—but it was not for sale till several years after I saw it and who can exile for oneself a ceiling? A far worse case occurred nearer home—a minute eighteenth-century castle outside Bath, once known as Connolly's folly. It was built in 1773 in the shape of the ace of clubs with three rooms on three floors, all circular, the ground and first floor stuccoed, with an octagonal hall on each landing. The arms of the Connolly owners (the same as my own) were over the door and on the glass in some windows and on the door of the small chapel, the stables were a replica of a convent with clock tower in miniature. There was a small gothic orangery, a tea pagoda in a wood, a gothic lodge, a lime avenue, and about sixty acres of woods and fields overlooking a wooded valley. All for about £8,000—which I had in the bank from a legacy. But I was on my own at the time and unable to take the plunge. The Bath suburbs were getting very close; the railway ran in full view. (How could I tell it would be discontinued?) And though I had the capital to buy it, I never seemed to possess even the fare to get down there. Sitting in our club, Evelyn Waugh assured me it was full of dry rot. He afterwards remembered he had confused it with somewhere else. The thought of propping up all that masonry, which seemed carved out of solid rock, appalled me, and I happened to be away when the agent, in despair, rang me up. Getting no answer, he sold it to a speculator who sold off the land and the timber, leaving only the beautiful shell to be bought by a richer and braver man than me. For the boom had by now set in, and if I could not have afforded to live in the home of my pseudo-ancestors, I could have sold it for a fortune. I know now that with houses, as with love, "We have all heard the key turn in the lock only once." Once the fatal instinct asserts itself, the "quod petis hic est"—"This is the place *for me*"—one should act on it forthwith and let no consideration of expense or convenience deter us, provided we can pay the deposit, nor must we fear loneliness, for a beautiful house will either attract a partner or prove a substitute for one. The awful daring of a moment's surrender. Now it is my punishment to inhabit a seaside villa built in 1886, consulting books on architecture.

Yet there is hope. England, in particular, is surprisingly rich in pavilions, though not as rich as France. One came up for sale not long ago, Luttrell's Tower, in the grounds of a house near Southampton, overlooking the Solent. The tower was built in 1730 by Simon Temple Luttrell, third son of Lord Carhampton of "Luttrellstown," Dublin. It may have been intended for brandy smuggling and has a flight of ornamental steps from the cellars to the shore. There is a fair-sized room on each of the three floors with bay windows and gothic panes looking over to the Isle of Wight, above a grove of evergreen oak; one is reminded of the Desert de Retz. I think the desire to possess one is stronger in England because so few pavilions are official. The royal palaces of the right period, Kew, Hampton Court, Kensington, produce only a pagoda between them. On the other hand there are many small country houses, of which Chiswick and Mereworth are examples, which could almost be called pavilions (Ebberston Hall in Yorkshire by Colin Campbell, architect of Mereworth, is another) and innumerable follies and grotesques, which could never be lived in—eye-catchers, hermit's grottoes, castellated barns, glorified ice-houses, summerhouses, and game larders. Carne's Seat, built in 1743 by Roger Morris for the tutor of the Duke of Richmond in the Park at Goodwood, is a true example; the shell grotto there, decorated in the 1740's, is not.

But first place among English pavilions must certainly be taken by Brighton's, the only one to have been a royal palace in its own right. The true test of a "maison de plaisance" is that it should

still give pleasure. The moment one crosses the threshold,
or even sees it from a distance, there should be an instant excitement
and satisfaction, a delight in detail, a sense of well-being, of
the invisible presence of talented precursors, the calm expertise of the
architect, the restrained enthusiasm of his patron, the
delight of his children, the satisfaction of his staff. The cellar fills with
Rhine and Constantia, with Margaux, ale, and sillery; the
silver room with Paul Storb; the display cabinets with Sevres and
Meissen or the local factories' products if you are in
Germany—the C.C.'s of Ludwigsbourg, the K.T.'s of Karl Theodor,
the shield of Nymphenburg, the F. of Frankenthal, the
sceptre of Berlin. The looking glasses and chandeliers are raised, the
tiled stoves and specially made furniture moved in. Only the
books are wanting, for I have yet to hear of a pavilion with a good
library. In vain do we imagine ourselves as a former
incumbent. He would quickly smell an intellectual, or worse, apply
the punishments of his time—the stocks or the galleys; the
pet-names vanish from his lips to be replaced by the icy third person,
unless we can produce our card, king-size and dripping with
rococo ornament.

The Royal Pavilion has all these requirements; it is one of
the happiest spots on this earth (I have known it all my life), and in
the summer months the tables are laid with fantastic vermeil
from the Londonderry collection; the kitchens with their spits and
casseroles arranged like organ pipes seem about to burst into
life. One must read the memoirs of Princess Lieven to discover how
deadly dull it was there with the Regent getting fuddled
every night on liqueurs.

The original pavilion was converted from a farmhouse by
Henry Holland for Mrs. Fitzherbert, whom the Prince of Wales had
secretly married in 1785. This "Marine Pavilion" was not
noticeably oriental. That note was supplied by the stables in 1804–88,
which echoed Cockerell's Mohammedan-Indian-style house
in Gloucestershire at Sezincote. By 1802 the Prince had redecorated
Holland's interiors with chinoiserie. In 1805 Humphrey
Repton submitted some drawings for an Indian pavilion, but when

money was eventually available John Nash was chosen. He
rebuilt the pavilion from 1815 to 1822 as it is now. The interior has
had much of the original furniture put back and all the
original wall decorations renewed. Everything compared with the
Amalienburg is on a course and elephantine; the music room
and banqueting room are in the Chinese style, the chimney pieces
Victorian, the main chandelier cost nearly six thousand
pounds and weighs a ton. "Everything impresses by cost and by
weight" (Nikolaus Pevsner). George IV never returned there
after 1822. The bedrooms, by the way, are delightful and simply
furnished. The last word must yet be with Pevsner, as always.

> It is this combination of Rococo and Victorian that sends us. We
> may well laugh at first, but then a feeling of intoxication will
> follow. There is in the end a great release in looking at and walking
> about in this folly, and so we stop asking questions.

The autumn is the best time for visiting pavilions. Water
and fallen leaves become them better than spring flowers; they belong
to the world of the hunt—"les souvenirs sont cor de chasse."

It was then that I set out on a piece of field-work with my
collaborator. We visited Stowe, now a great public school
whose grounds are festooned with follies and grottoes. These are bare
inside and besides being too well known somehow just fall
outside our definition, for none to the best of my knowledge has slept
in them. Only the two Boycott pavilions, (a pair of small
lodges) are habitable. They are by James Gibbs, and the designs were
published by him in 1729. These "rusticated cubes,"
guardians of the vanished hamlet of Boycott, once carried octagonal
steeples, replaced in 1758 by domes. They are enchanting.
Apart from the temples—of Friendship, of Ancient Virtue (William
Kent's masterpiece), of Concord and Victory, and the shrine
of the British worthies—there are two real dwellings: the "Queens
Temple" by J. F. Blondel (1773–74), a nephew of the great
French architect, a typical small classical building (now the music
school) with a pedimented portico of four Corinthian
columns, and Gibbs's "Gothic Building" of 1744 of golden
Northamptonshire iron-stone. It is a most unusual triangular
building, originally dedicated to Liberty; its turrets and gables enclose

a circular gallery beneath a traceried dome, and the
windows were filled with stained glass. I preferred the little obelisk
erected by Lord Cobham in memory of his friend Congreve,
a monkey perched on a rustic pyramid regarding himself in a mirror.
The whole ensemble of Stowe is a monument to Whig
humanism, political gardening, and the cult of wisdom through the
best architects—"sapientum templa serena."

Our travels next brought us to Northamptonshire, via the "Chinese"
rooms of the Verney family at Claydon, then the Hawksmoor
splendours of Eastern Neston. (Hawksmoor's mausoleum at Castle
Howard in Yorkshire, one of the most beautiful of all small
buildings, is by definition a home for the dead, not the living.)

Finally, we came to a true pavilion, indeed two of them,
approached through a wood at Stoke Bruern. The twin pavilions and
colonnades once formed part of a larger house in the center
which was begun but never finished by Sir Francis Crane, the man
who established the seventeenth-century Mortlake Tapestry.
He brought the design from Italy, and in the execution of it received
the assistance of Inigo Jones. The design may have been
taken from Vignola's Villa, Papa Giulio. The two are at present lived
in by Mr. Chancellor, a pavilion-lover of the true lineage,
and form, with their large water basin, one of the most beautiful
dwellings in England. One pavilion has a library, the other
the bedrooms; they are tall for their size and belong, with the great
Venetian windows, to the purest style of the English
Renaissance, with something grand about them, like Greenwich or
Christchurch Library. The water basin, as at Easton Neston,
completes the picture with its views of the blue Northamptonshire
skyline.

We then departed for the West, stopping to see Lord Sherborne's
hunting box in a Cotswold forest, a "pavillon de chasse" not
very common in England, before reaching our final quarry, Frampton
Court, on the Severn. The classical north front with its flight
of steps, pediment, and four Ionic pilasters is typically Palladian
(1731–33), but the garden at the back contains an exquisite

Gothic garden house at the end of a wide canal (1760). It consists of a pair of conjoined octagons with an octagon turret above, topped by a small cupola. It has remained in the Clifford family, who have lived at Frampton for many centuries, passing in 1684 through the female line to the Clutterbucks. The windows of the garden house (used as a dower house by the family) are particularly romantic as is the elaborate water setting.

Of all water and wood combinations, the most beautiful is Stourhead. The National Trust has now planted back the rhododendrons that were destroying its formality and set them to colour the sheltering woods. "One of the most picturesque scenes in the world," Horace Walpole called it. "All gardening is landscape painting," said Alexander Pope, and Stourhead is based on Claude and Salvator Rosa. The temples are set round an irregular artificial lake, and Miss Masson thinks that the banker Hoare may even have got his idea of composing a lake-landscape from Pliny's description of the source of the Clitumnus. The grotto, with its nymph and river god, bears this out. Then comes Henry Flitcroft's evocation of the Pantheon and last, on the other side of the lake, the circular "Temple of the Sun" with its domed rotunda (1765) by Flitcroft. It is derived from the temple of Venus at Baalbec in one of the most satisfactory of all shapes.

One must mention two more northern pavilions near the adjoining monasteries of Fountains Abbey and Rievaulx in Yorkshire. At Studley Royal is the Banque House attributed to Colin Campbell and Roger Morris, and at Dunscombe, on a high stretch of turf above Rievaulx, are two pavilions in one of which the Earls of Feversham entertained and seated royalty down to the present day. There is a circular Tuscan temple and an Ionic temple, fully furnished for the feast. This last is a particularly delightful building with its stretch of green galloping turf and its views of the ruined abbey and the moors.

SWEDEN

ROSENDAHL

Rosendahl, the Royal Pavilion in
Stockholm on the South Bjurgarden, was designed by the
architect Fredrik Rikblom, and was erected between 1823 and 1827. It
was built especially for Karl XIV Johann, the first Bernadotte
King, whose wife was Dessire, and for Oscar II. Used by the Royal
Family as a "maison de plaisance" until 1913, it was then
opened as the Bernadotte Museum.

The somewhat severe front facade is embellished with a
one-story Ionic-columned portico. The building is distinctly in the
neoclassic tradition.

The interior is richly decorated with damask walls, and classic friezes,
and is filled with an impressive collection of furniture and
paintings of the period.

A smaller wooden house is attached and is consistent in
interior décor and furnishings with the main pavilion.

GUNNEBO

Gunnebo, as it stands today, was erected between 1784 and 1796, during King Gustavus's reign. It was built for John Hall, Sr., a Gothenburg merchant of Scottish extraction, by Carl Wilhelm Carlberg. The architect not only designed the buildings and the garden, but the fixtures, wall décor, stoves, and furniture as well. The sculpture is by the Italian Gioachimo Frulli.

The handsome drawing room on the main floor is done in the most restrained neoclassic taste, with columns, reliefs, and life-sized sculptures of classical figures set in niches. The ceiling is decorated with the more flamboyant swags and putti.

The neoclassical exterior of the building has a peristyle with Ionic columns on the north facade. The south facade was originally adorned with a big balcony and a flight of steps leading to the two sides. A lead relief depicting genii gathering grapes is inserted in the facade.

After passing through many hands, the building was carefully restored by the late Baron and Baroness Carl Sparre. The estate is currently a Swedish National Trust Monument, in the care of a special board chosen by the Molndal Town Council.

GUSTAV III'S PAVILION AT HAGA

Gustav III's Pavilion at Haga (1787–89) was built from the designs of Olaf Temperman in close collaboration with the King himself. However, despite the French character of the exterior, it is the interior—by Louis Masreliez, a Swede of French extraction—which speaks of genius.

The arabesques and figures, which form the basic motif of the panels and friezes in the large drawing room, derive from the classic Roman and Italian Renaissance periods. Graeco-Roman gods in the Raphael manner are to be found everywhere, as well as designs from the baths of Titus and Pompeii. It is evident that the decorator rejected much of the ubiquitous French influence in favor of the neoclassic.

A cast of Johan Tobias Sergel's medallion of the poet Gustav Philip Cruetz, Swedish Ambassador in Paris at the time, and the man responsible for the superb book collection, hangs over the marble fireplace in the library.

A number of smaller pavilions are to be found on the grounds, including the Turkish Pavilion (1786–88) and the Chinese Pavilion (1787).

28

SWEDEN

CHINESE PAVILION, DROTTINGHOLM

The Chinese Pavilion at Drottingholm
was originally built in 1753 as a surprise birthday present for
Queen Louisa Ulrika on her thirty-fourth birthday by her husband,
King Adolf Frederick. It was secretly constructed of wood in
Stockholm and then shipped by water to its present site. The existing
pavilion, a more permanent structure, was built in 1769 and
adds a romantic note to the strict symmetry of the baroque structures
at the estate.

Throughout the pavilion, the Oriental motif dominates, reflecting the
Chinese mode, which seized Europe during the
mid-eighteenth century. Lacquered panels from Japan adorn the walls,
Chinese porcelain vases and urns of the eighteenth century
are to be found everywhere. Furniture is covered in Chinese silk. The
"Red Cabinet" is an imitation of a Cantonese interior.

The upper story includes a "whispering room," where an intimate
word passed to a wall is echoed to the listener's ear on the
other side of the room.

THE HOVMARSKALKINNAN'S PAVILION AT SVINDERSVIK

The Svindersvik estate proper was a gift of King Gustavas Vasa to the Davidens Hospital (an asylum). In 1636 it reverted to the Crown and was transferred to a Dutchman named van Swindern; hence its name. Within the complex is the Hovmarskalkinnan's Pavilion, a superb example of the eighteenth-century Gustavian style, a Swedish adaptation of Louis Quatorze. The building has several interesting architectural features, including a narrow L-shaped outer section of brick built in the 1770's, and an octagonal entry hall of wood, which was added later. Another addition, quite different in style, is a drawing room constructed of wood.

A painting by Carl Petter Hilleström, a well-known Swedish artist, done in 1784, shows the pavilion as it looked before the extensive alterations were made. These were executed to provide proper accommodations for a great ball given in honor of King Gustav III, a frequent visitor to the fashionable light suppers held at the pavilion after theater.

The interior décor is a mixture of classical motifs and rococo elements, complemented by a simple pearl-gray furniture. The French spirit is felt throughout—truly elegant and timeless in its appeal. The Hovmarskalkinnan's Pavilion is open to the public under the auspices of the Nordik Museum.

SWEDEN

DENMARK
THE HERMITAGE

THE HERMITAGE

The Hermitage, a Royal Hunting
Lodge in the Deer Park north of Copenhagen, was built in
1734–36, during the reign of Christian VI. The Royal Master Mason,
Laurids de Thurah, was commissioned to design the building
to replace one which had grown a bit dog-eared through neglect,
during the reign of Christian V.

A sphinx-flanked staircase leads to the entrance of the mansard-roofed
pavilion. In keeping with the function of the building, the
main story is embellished with sandstone mythological, sylvan dieties
set in niches and a portrait in relief of Christian VI.

The walls of the central dining hall, on the first floor, are divided by
artificial marble pilasters. Marble portals and fireplace are
set with reliefs on a background of mirrors. The ceiling is embellished
with Royal monograms and multicolored stucco reliefs of
hunting gear, with mirror inserts.

Originally, a table which could be lowered by a lift to the
kitchen was placed in the hall so that the Royal party could dine
without servants to wait on them.

I am deeply grateful to Her Majesty the Queen for permitting me to
photograph the interior.

DENMARK

RUSSIA

THE PAVILIONS AT TSARSKOE SELO
THE AGATE PAVILION
THE CHINESE PAVILION
THE GROTTO
THE CATHERINE PAVILION
THE MONTAIGNE RUSSE AT ORANIENBAUM

THE PAVILIONS AT TSARKOE SELO

THE AGATE
THE CHINESE PAVILION
THE GROTTO
THE CATHERINE PAVILION

Although the French and Italian influences on Russian taste are generally recognized, few people are aware of the great influence which England had in Russia during the Petersburgian period (1770–1820) in particular. Charles Cameron, a Scottish architect, little known in the British Isles even today, was the architect selected by Catherine the Great to redecorate her apartments at Tsarskoe Selo and to build the Agate Pavilion and Colonnade.

Built between 1782–85, the Agate Pavilion, a bath pavilion, has a semicircular Ionic gallery joining two wings. On the garden side the facade is Italian, of a rustic style resembling Giulio Romano and Michele Sanmicheli. A ramp was included so that the aging Empress Catherine could be wheeled in.

The interior décor is largely a mixture of the Greek and Italian. The ground floor contains hot and cold baths, largely carried out in white marble with gilded bronze decoration, all adapted from Roman models.

The first floor contains the Agate Room, the Jasper Room, and four smaller rooms. Here Cameron had the assistance of English workmen and of the sculptors Flaxman and Rachette. The first small room, or Blue Room, is particularly beautiful, as the stools, couches, and enormous vases are rendered in the same style, material, and color as the walls.

The round "cabinet de toilette" is pink and gold. In the Great Hall, pink and white marble are blended and adorned with gilded bronze. The antechamber is jasper and agate, while the Jasper Room is divided by a portico with an entablature supported by columns and pilasters of solid red agate.

In addition to the Agate Pavilion, the grounds of the palace also contain other pavilions of an earlier date. One of these is the delightful Chinese Pavilion, which was used as a teahouse by the Imperial Family. It is set in the park on the road to the Chinese Village which was never completed.

Evidently the Imperial Family liked to take tea frequently, as a Grotto was also built to be used as a teahouse.

Another pavilion, the Hermitage, was built for Catherine by the Italian architect Bartolemmeo Rastrelli in 1746. It was planned as the center of a projected garden of topiary work. It consists of four projecting wings around a central room, whose upper floor was a banqueting hall. The charming interior designs were by Valeriani. This is the one remaining building on the grounds which has yet to be restored.

The Agate Pavilion

The Catherine Pavilion

The Chinese Pavilion

The Grotto

The Catherine Pavilion

THE MONTAIGNE RUSSE AT ORANIENBAUM

The Montaigne Russe, or Tobaggan Pavilion, at Oranienbaum, now called Lomonosov, was designed by Antonio Rinaldi in 1760. The handsome blue-and-white building was the launching pad for a five-hundred-yard wooden track supported by 763 pillars. This enabled the Royal party to enjoy a swift and invigorating toboggan ride to the bottom. The slide collapsed in 1858 and was not rebuilt.

The interior "chinoiserie" is by the Italians, Torelli and the Berozzi brothers.

RUSSIA

HOLLAND

TROMPENBURG
OVER HOLLAND
GUNTERSTEIN

TROMPENBURG

The country estate of Trompenburg
was originally constructed by Admiral Cornelius Tromp. The
French had demolished part of it in 1672, and the restoration was
completed during the latter part of the seventeenth century.

The precise, rectangular, neoclassical living quarters are impressive,
however, and it is the octagonal domed structure connected
to it by a corridor which is unique. The admiral planned it to give him
the impression that he was still on a ship of the fleet.

The dome, completely surrounded by water, is derivative of the Huis
Tem Bosch near The Hague. The exterior is flanked by four
three-story pedimented bays. Sculptures are placed in niches near
the base of the structure.

The interior is elaborately decorated with painted ceiling and walls
utilizing the Ionic motif.

The building is now owned and maintained by the Dutch government.

51

OVER HOLLAND

Over Holland was built in 1676 and
was in its time one of the greatest buildings on the Vecht.
Its name has a peculiar derivation, for it at one time was across the
river from the territory of Holland, hence Over Holland.

The famous Swedish botanist Linnaeus conducted much of his
research here. And for many years, the pavilion was owned
by Jacob Poppen of Amsterdam, the richest merchant of his era.

The novelist Van Zeggelen lived at Over Holland for three
months in summer residence, and wrote in his well-known novel
de Plaetse aan de Vecht about Poppen and his ten
lovely daughters.

It is presently owned and maintained by the Utreschtsch
Landschap, who have restored it to its present excellent state.

GUNTERSTEIN

The castle of Gunterstein stands on the foundations of an earlier one destroyed by the French troops in 1673. In 1680 a Huguenot widow from Calais, Magdalena Poulle, decided to rebuild the house. For one built by a woman, it is extremely masculine, and is unlike the other Dutch country houses along the Vecht River.

There is a portrait of her nephew, aged three, who laid the foundation stone, holding the plan of the house in his hand.

In 1823 two semicircular porticos with balconies were added. They are a great asset, softening the severity of the house. There is a small tower on the roof with statues in niches on its four sides. The tower hides the chimney stacks.

56

Rosendahl, the Royal Pavilion in Stockholm, Sweden

Château de La Gaude, near Aix-en-Provence, France

The Badenburg at Nymphenburg Palace, Munich, Germany

The Hermitage, a Royal Hunting Lodge, north of Copenhagen, Denmark

Stoke Park, one of two pavilions, at Towcaster, England.

The Marino Casino, high on a hill overlooking Dublin Bay, Ireland

BELGIUM

BELVEDERE

BELVEDERE

Belvedere, an eighteenth-century "folie," is situated in the park surrounding the Royal Palace at Laeken, Brussels, Belgium. Crown Prince Albert and Princess Paola of Belgium live there.

Located on a small artificial hill, the neoclassical structure was built in 1788 for the banker Vicomte de Waliers by the architect Payen and the Frenchman Montoyer. The interior is rendered in the purest neo-Pompeian manner, while the exterior is distinctly derived from Palladio.

The pavilion passed through several hands until finally it became the property of the Belgian Royal Family, who have exquisitely restored it, the only change being an early addition of a pepper-pot dome, and a service pavilion across from the entrance porte-cochère.

GERMANY
SCHLOSS BENRATH
SOLITUDE

SCHLOSS BENRATH

Benrath, not far from Düsseldorf, is a pavilion only in the sense that its central core is one, the enormous outbuildings creating a château or palace. However, the pale-pink core, with its blue-gray-tiled, mansard-roofed terminating ends, have all the essence and charm that the early-eighteenth-century French school gave to German architecture. It is for these reasons that it is included in this book.

Built for Elector Karl Theodor by Nicolas de Pigage from Lorraine, near Lunéville, where former King Stanislaus of Poland held court, Benrath appears to be a two-story "maison de plaisance." Actually, it is four stories in height, with apartments for the gentlemen and ladies-in-waiting opening onto interior courtyards, and those for domestics on a floor above. Even the chimneys are unobtrusive from the exterior.

Across a large pond from the town's main road, the complete compound, with the enormous service wings, is in view. One of these includes the kitchens attached to the main pavilion by an underground passage. The other three sides also overlook water, but are planted in a more intimate manner. The most impressive is on the garden side, where the oval salon overlooks a long pool.

The interiors are gay, light, and delightful. Regretfully the Elector had little chance to enjoy it as he had many other homes, and for political reasons lived largely in Munich. The building, badly damaged during the war, has been expertly restored.

64

SOLITUDE

Karl-Eugen, Duke of Württemberg, came upon a place known as "The Five Oaks" deep in the forest near Stuttgart during a hunt. The site, with its great views of the Franconian Mountains and the foothills of the Vosges, inspired him to commission the architect La Guepière to design Solitude. In four years (1760–64) the castle rose, a single-storied block with a gilded dome reached by a horseshoe staircase.

The interior is dominated by a huge oval hall, probably used as a dining hall. Its walls are decorated with double Ionic columns. The ceiling is the work of Guibal. Beautiful stuccoes by Bossi embellish the entire pavilion.

In its heyday, Solitude was the site of many extravagant galas. A thousand bonfires would light the surrounding hills, and artificial grottos were brought to life with myriads of nymphs and dancing satyrs. There were, however, times when the place reverted to an atmosphere more in keeping with its name. During these periods, the court assumed that the Duke was undoubtedly involved in yet another "affaire de coeur."

GERMANY

BAVARIA

LINDERHOF
THE AMALIENBURG AT NYMPHENBURG PALACE
THE PAGODENBURG AT NYMPHENBURG PALACE
THE BADENBURG AT NYMPHENBURG PALACE

LINDERHOF

One wish most cherished by Louis II of
Bavaria was to emulate the splendor and magnificence of the
Bourbons, who in his eyes, incarnated absolute monarchy directed by
the right hand of God. It is for this reason that he
adopted the sun emblem of Louis XIV for his personal use and the
architectural style of Versailles at Linderhof.

Set in a quiet valley in the serene forested foothills of the Bavarian
Alps, Linderhof was designed by the architect Georg
Dollman. Work on the château began in 1874; it was completed in
1878. The two-story villa is in the French eighteenth-century
style evoking not the Petit Trianon of Marie Antoinette, whom Louis
greatly admired, but a birthday cake. The impressive facade
is ornamented with balustrades and sculptures set in niches. It is
almost too much, but in its fantasy one finds charm.

The gardens of Linderhof recall their Italian and French prototypes,
with splendid terraces, fountains, and sculptures. A vast
park in the English manner is also on the grounds, and it is here that
the Grotto of Venus is located. It represents the first-act
Venusberg scene from Wagner's opera *Tannhäuser*. A Moorish
pavilion is also in this area, all quite mad and full of fantasy,
like the King himself.

The interior includes a grand bedroom, a hall of mirrors,
and a music room resplendent with Gobelin tapestries depicting
shepherds and the bucolic life so dear to the
eighteenth-century French taste.

THE AMALIENBURG AT NYMPHENBURG PALACE

The Amalienburg, named after Electress Maria Amalie, was the last of the pavilions to be added to the summer residence complex. Serving as a hunting lodge, it was built during the years 1734–39.

Over the entrance to the one-story domed building, Diana, Goddess of the Hunt, and sylvan creatures are depicted. Busts of friendly satyrs fill the niches.

The interior includes a "hundekammer," or dog room. Here the spaniels could pause in their dog houses beneath the gun cupboards to chew on an old bone or two before getting down to serious hunting. The kitchen is done in colored Delft, which depicts Chinese flowers and everyday scenes.

The building was conceived by Cuvilliés, the Elder, a court dwarf, who was trained as an architect in Paris. The interior is considered one of the finest extant examples of secular Bavarian baroque architecture.

The oval drawing room in blue and silver is one of the most beautiful rooms in the world, and is complemented by the yellow and silver rooms on each side.

A small stairway leads to a vantage point on the roof for watching the hunt.

72

THE PAGODENBURG
AT NYMPHENBURG
PALACE

The Pagodenburg was the first of the
pleasure pavilions to be erected in the gardens of
Nymphenburg Palace, summer residence of the rulers of Bavaria.

Elector Max Emanuel had been exiled in France and while
there picked up the taste for the Chinese style in vogue in Paris at the
time. In 1716, when he returned to Munich, he built his
teahouse in the Chinese manner.

Since Oriental china was unavailable, and since domestic
china was only beginning to be manufactured, he decorated the walls
and staircase of the pavilion with Delft faience tiles.

On the upper floor, the rooms are decorated with panels of
red-and-black lacquer paintings, Oriental wallpaper and
lacquered veneer furniture from Paris.

THE BADENBURG AT NYMPHENBURG PALACE

Teahouses are all well and good, but a
palace simply isn't a palace without a bathhouse. And so,
construction of the Badenburg took place during the years 1718–21.
Here, the whole royal gang could splash in the
blue-and-white Delft-tiled pool, and watch Hercules throw rocks at
the water nymphs, or Leda and that dirty old swan up on
the ceiling.

After the dip, perhaps a sit-down dinner in the large
two-storied baroque stucco-ornamented banquet hall would be in
order, or even a short stop in the bedrooms, meticulously
done in Chinese wallpaper painted with "life-sized Indian figures."

ITALY

THE VILLA LANTE, BAGNAIA

The Villa Lante is not one house, but
rather twin "casinos" set in one of the loveliest of all
Italian gardens.

Cardinal Gambera, the Bishop of Viterbo, built it in 1564 as
his summer home. His successor, Cardinal Montalto, finished the
garden, which later still, came into the possession of the
Lante family, from which it takes its name.

A natural stream from the hill above was trained to course
through this most formal of gardens, terminating in a central fountain
where young stone boys hold up the Montalto coat of arms,
a star which is made up of jets of water.

VILLA MASER VOLPI (BARBARO)

Charming on its exterior, the Villa is most famous for its superb interior decoration, largely the work of Paolo Veronese. Palladio was the architect. It was built between 1560 and 1568.

The interior walls are painted with trompe-l'oeil scenes of ruins and of statues in niches. For architectural balance, there are two painted doors with life-size human figures before them, wearing costumes of the period. One is supposed to be of Veronese's mistress, the other of himself. There is also a painted balcony with figures leaning over to see what is going on below. The figures are of members of the Barbaro family and their pets.

The garden room, where these murals are, is the most beautiful room in the villa, and opens onto a semicircular garden, with a pool and a grotto with a pair of outscale Neptune-like figures. This little garden is set against the hillside.

87

ITALY

VILLA CORDELLINA (LOMBARDI)

The most striking feature of the facade of this villa is its impressive Ionic-columned portico, which, though recessed, seems to stand out because of its massive round columns and commanding pediment. The architect, Giorgio Massari (1686–1766), was obviously inspired by Palladio. The dependencies, however, are done in the style of Baldassarre Longhena.

Begun in 1735, the villa was finally completed in 1760. In the grand reception hall, there are three superb frescos painted by Tiepolo in 1743. For years Villa Cordellina (now called Villa Lombardi) was neglected and fell into a state of serious decay. Fortunately, it has recently been restored to its former magnificence.

LOGGIA IN SALVI GARDEN, VICENZA

The Loggetta in the Salvi Garden, also known as the Loggetta Valmarana, was constructed by Antonio Palladio and commissioned by Leonardo Valmarana. This rather democratic gentleman opened the gardens to the public in the year 1592.

Just above the water, which lies before the loggia, are five arches which support the balustraded first floor. Six Doric columns support the entablature and the pedimented roof.

A beautiful Latin inscription is engraved above the main entrance arch: *Hilaritati ac genio dicata* or "Abandon yourself to laughter and insouciance."

VILLA ROTONDA

The Villa Rotonda, or Villa Almerico Capra, near Vicenza was originally designed for Monsignor Paolo Almerico, Referendary to Popes Pius IV and V, for his old-age retirement. Sold in 1589 by his illegitimate son to the Capra Brothers, it was completed by Vincenzo Scamozzi. Probably, the building was commenced in the late 1560's. A debate has raged for centuries as to the extent of Scamozzi's modifications from the original Palladian plan. The primary controversy is over the fact that the dome in Palladio's drawings is considerably higher than the existing one.

Truly the most famous of Palladio's villas, and a milestone in architectural history, Villa Rotonda is particularly admired for the harmony achieved between the design of the building and its site. As far back as the seventeenth century it was a tourist stop.

Its influence ranged to the British Isles, where no less than four versions of it exist: Chiswick, Mereworth, Footscray, and Nuttall Temple, as well as to the United States and to Russia. The villa is presently owned by Conte Andrea di Valmarana, whose family has lived in it for centuries.

THE PALACE
GARDEN CASINO
AT STRA

At Stra, on the Riviera del Brenta between Venice and Padua, is located the very impressive Villa Pisani. The main building is in the neoclassic style of the eighteenth century and is reminiscent of Palladio. The roof cornice is replete with many statues, both sacred and profane.

The interior of the villa contains many noteworthy paintings, including frescoes by Jacopa Guarana.

The gardens include a labyrinth, stables, and the little garden casino. Atop the balustraded roof cornice, a series of statues carry out the style of the villa itself.

THE BOBOLI BELVEDERE, FLORENCE

The gardens of the Pitti Palace are almost as famous as the palace itself. They extend on a hill site, which goes up from the main axis. There is an outdoor amphitheater of considerable beauty, and beyond the hill a rise to a fountain terminus. The major position of the gardens extends downward to the right of the palace. There are dark avenues of plane trees, or hornbeam, cut into high hedges, a delightful water garden known as the Isolotto, and a superb allée of cypress.

Since the space is quite limited, the treatment of the garden on the left side of the palace is simple. There on the hillside is a small belvedere, which Cardinal Leopoldo de Medici built.

Although secluded on two sides, it has an excellent view of the city. It has one large, high-ceilinged room with painted trellis, flowers, and birds, and a painted sky above. It was most likely used as a teahouse, and even today one may buy cold drinks and enjoy the view from its terrace.

FOSCARI ("LA MALCONTENTA"), NEAR VENICE

Built in 1560 for Nicolò and Luigi de Foscari, with Andrea Palladio as the architect, it was not completed until 1571. It is placed close to the Brenta Canal, not far from Venice. Its situation in a section known for its mists—even on a sunny day—accounts for its nickname "La Malcontenta."

Its superb frescoes by C. B. Franco and G. B. Zelotti were stripped from most of its walls during its period of decay, but not too faint and evocative traces of them still are visible.

VILLA VALMARANA

Valmarana, also known as Villa dei Nani, was begun in 1669 by the Muttoni family. It was sold in the eighteenth century to the Valmarana family, who commissioned Tiepolo to do the frescoes, for which it is famous. There is one room which is especially lovely, with its frescoes in the Chinese manner.

On the high wall along the road are figures of dwarfs, and the legend is that one of the villa's owners had a daughter who was a dwarf. To hide the fact from her, he employed only dwarfs as servants, and had the sculptured figures of them made to top the wall. Unfortunately one day, from an upper window, she saw a handsome prince and his companions ride by, and realizing the truth, killed herself.

ITALY

CAPRARIOLA, THE CASINO OF THE VILLA FARNESE

This delightful villa, or casino, which is now the summer residence of the President of Italy, is placed on a hillside behind the austere bulk of the Villa Farnese. It was built as an escape from the cold formality of its parent villa.

The casino and its garden were finished in 1587, and remain much today as they were originally. One approaches the casino by a path through woods, so when one comes to it, it is a pleasant surprise. The open loggia has a fresco of gardens and country, quite in keeping with its light-hearted ambience.

FRANCE

PAVILLON L'ENFANT, AIX-EN-PROVENCE
CHÂTEAU DE LA GAUDE, NEAR AIX
REYNERY, NEAR TOULOUSE
MALLE, NEAR BORDEAUX
HÔTEL SAINT-MARC, BORDEAUX
FOLIE DES FRÈRES LABOTTIÈRE, BORDEAUX
CHÂTEAU DE LA GATAUDIÈRE, CHARENTE-MARITIME
MANOR OF VONNE
CHÂTEAU D'ORMESSON
BOUGES
CHÂTEAU DES GROTTEAUX, NEAR CHAMBORD
BAGATELLE AT ABBEVILLE
BEAUMONT-SUR-VINGEANNE
LA BECHELLERIE, NEAR TOURS

PAVILLON L'ENFANT, AIX-EN-PROVENCE

At the gates of the city of Aix stands the gracious seventeenth-century Pavillon de L'Enfant. Beautiful gardens, shaded by rows of one-hundred-year-old chestnut and linden trees surround the villa, and a large pool and fountain dominate the main terrace.

The square pavilion's three-story facade looks over the water of the pond. Each story has three windows, and in the center is a large door of carved wood, dating from around 1675. The corners of the roof are decorated with chimneys and a sun dial is affixed to the facade.

Built by Rambot, one of the architects of the Vendôme, and by the sculptor Tauro, it was commissioned by Simon de L'Enfant, Treasurer General of France (1616–93). The family owned L'Enfant until 1795, when the last surviving male died. It was left to the Cathedral of Saint-Sauveur d'Aix. In 1955, a doctor, M. Dieulangard, acquired it from Saint-Seige.

The original fireplaces, sculpted by Tauro, still stand in the small salon and the dining room. Marble fountains and delicately sculpted silver by Tauro decorate the corners.

From the vestibule, an impressive staircase leads to the second story. Frescos attributed to Van Loo include, "An Assembly of the Gods" on the oval ceiling and "The Court of Apollo and the Arts" in the grand salon.

CHÂTEAU DE LA GAUDE, NEAR AIX

La Gaude, built around 1700, is a small château located near Aix-en-Provence. It fits exactly the description of a "folie." Charles François Joseph Pisani de La Gaude, after whom the pavilion is named, wished to offer it as a worthy token of his love to a young girl who was to be his wife. However, his beloved died on their wedding night. The inconsolable de La Gaude, a counselor to Parliament from Provence, took leave of worldly life and entered a monastery, eventually becoming Bishop of Vence.

Perhaps the primary charm of La Gaude is the magnificent perspective of the garden, descending in many terrace levels and looking out over the range of l'Étoile. The first terrace, set between two great pools of water and ornamented with vases and fountains, contains a boxwood maze whose bushes are over two hundred years old. Sculptures of sea dogs and a dauphin by Chastel adorn the main terrace. A circular pool occupies the third terrace, which looks out onto a border of yews and cypress trees. On the side, a small Louis XVI chapel stands behind a fountain, which spurts nine jets of water.

The house itself is constructed of light buff-colored stone, and consists of three stories, each with five windows. A pediment graces the top of the central core. Until recently, the interior was unfortunately in disrepair, having been changed frequently over the years. La Gaude is owned by the Baron de Vitrolles.

REYNERY,
NEAR TOULOUSE

Close to Toulouse, ancient city of
bricks, pink and soft of color, lies a property almost
unknown, and certainly forgotten. It is the farm of Reynery, a working
farm that encircles and all but ignores the beautiful "folie"
that is its raison d'être. "Folie," yes, too small for a château, too
beautiful and too important in detail to call a house.

Reynery was the home of Guillaume du Barry, the complaisant
husband of la du Barry, with whom he never lived. After
her execution, he married his mistress of many years, Madelaine
Lemoine, and they made Reynery their summer home.
Much of the original furniture survives.

A family dispute in court left Reynery unlived-in for some
time. Now the windows open once again, the grass is cut, the hedges
trimmed, the trees pruned and the "folie" once more is one
of the most seductive small houses in all of France. It belongs to
Mme. Ricard.

Reynery has tremendous water sources. The small stream through the
wash house flows swiftly, and the jet in the center
decorative pool never stops its play.

114

MALLE, NEAR BORDEAUX

Malle, located in the heart of the
Bordeaux country, has been carefully maintained since it
was erected, in the seventeenth century. Through marriage and
inheritance, it has passed through and among the Malle, de
Lur-Saluces, and the de Bournazel families, all of whom have added a
wing or two to the exterior with loving affection.

The interior has been respected through the centuries. It is replete
with marble floors, beamed ceilings, impressive marble
fireplaces, and the original furniture and paintings. There is still in
place the billiard table behind which the then Marquise
stood with her daughters when the revolutionaries came for her
husband. He at that moment was jumping his horse over a
brick wall and fleeing to Spain.

The pavilion, of Italian inspiration, is surrounded by
extensive grounds with many charming sculptures. Nymphs are to be
found here and there, as well as replicas of the personages of
the Commedia dell' Arte.

The view from the grand esplanade of Malle, is perhaps one
of the most impressive of the Sauterne country in the area.

The Count Pierre de Bournazel is the present owner, and
his vineyards produce a superior sauterne, which is much in demand.

HÔTEL SAINT-MARC, BORDEAUX

In the year 1773, the royal architect
of Louis XVI, Victor Louis, arrived in Bordeaux. Before long
his style, the neoclassic, dominated the architectural style of the city.

One fine example of his influence in design is the summer
house of the Marquis de Saint-Marc, who according to a plaque
placed on the building was not only a poet and playwright,
but a "collector" as well.

The building, the Hôtel Saint-Marc, is distinguished by the
front porch, which is crowned by a cupola supported by a colonnade
in the Ionic order. The Temple of Vesta in Rome was the
inspiration for this pavilion.

FOLIE DES FRÈRES LABOTTIÈRE, BORDEAUX

Another pavilion in the city of Bordeaux which shows the influence of Victor Louis is the Folie des Frères Labottière, built around 1775 by Étienne Laclotte, for the Labottière brothers, who were printers.

A glance at the neoclassical pavilion reveals an elevation crowned with an Italian balustrade. Garlands of fruit ornament the tops of the windows. A semicircular bay dominates the two-story center of the rear of the building.

The main entrance of the "folie" is flanked by two columns, over which a balustrade with two additional supporting columns stand.

CHÂTEAU DE LA GATAUDIÈRE, CHARENTE-MARITIME

This charming, modest-sized château was built in the early part of the eighteenth century by François Fresman, on his return from the South Pacific. He brought with him the rubber tree.

His daughter married in 1794 the future General de Chasseloup-Laubat, and their descendants still own the château, which is just as when it was built.

When I stopped to photograph the place, an old electric had driven in ahead of me (it was during the gasoline strike), and an elderly couple got out. I explained my mission, and the Marquis told me that I could of course take photos, but I must stay for lunch. I was delighted and I told them of my experiences taking photos at other châteaux, which amused them. The Marquise was unwell and left to lie down immediately after the meal. When I left, the Marquis came out to the car with me and thanked me for taking his wife's mind off herself.

122

MANOR OF VONNE

This ancient manor house is located
near the main road leading from Azay-le-Rideau to the town
of Artannes at Indre-et-Loire. It is now inhabited by a farmer, renting
it from the owner, who prefers a more modern house
nearby.

Dating from the sixteenth century, the house is entirely
built of dressed limestone of a warm gray color, carved in places.
Many of the large mullioned windows have been filled in
with rubble. The first time I saw it, only the great central room and
one other small room were in use. Hay and fodder filled the
rest of the rooms. Today it is being restored.

The right wing contains a simple circular stone staircase, and
the remains of an elaborately carved mantel. At the back of the house,
a high stoop of about fourteen steps leads to the main door;
while in the front one step is required to reach the door.

In addition to the excellent proportions of the building, it is
interesting as an example of work similar to, but smaller than,
Azay-le-Rideau. It also contains one room whose great carved
mantel is comparable to any in that royal house. The Manor of Vonne
is also similar in size and plan to Huisseau-sur-Cosson,
located some one hundred kilometers to the east and of a later date.

Vonne was romanticized by Honoré de Balzac as the model
for the imaginary Château de Clochegourd in his novel
Le Lys dans la Valle.

CHÂTEAU D'ORMESSON

Originally known as Château d'Ambiole, Ormesson was given by Henry IV to the wife of one of his financial advisors. The château later passed into the hands of the d'Ormesson family and assumed its name. The Princesse Bibesco exclaimed, upon seeing the château for the first time, "Narcissus-House"! Surrounded by water, it is connected to land by delicate stone footbridges. The gardens, laid out by Le Nôtre, sparkle with fountains and are guarded by adjoining woodlands.

The older part of the château, built around 1580, with its somewhat rustic facade, differs considerably from the more elegant eighteenth-century addition. The whole, however, is unified by the well-integrated roofs. The interior remains almost unchanged—with Louis XV panelling, over-doors painted in grisaille, graceful fireplaces, and parquet de Versailles.

Fortunately, Ormesson has remained in the family. Its present master is Comte Wladimir d'Ormesson of the Académie Française, onetime French Ambassador to the Holy See.

BOUGES

The existing house at Bouges was built
in 1759 by Charles-François Leblanc de Marnaval, who
bought the older château from Bertrand de La Tour,
the Count of Auvergne.

Marnaval, who was a rich industrialist, constructed the present building
after the designs of Gabriel on the ruins of the old château.
It was executed by the architect Fayeti, who put his signature on the
main pediment. The finest available talent was recruited
from Versailles to assist in the construction. Bouchardon did the
statues in the gardens, Coypel the overdoors, and Oudry the
décor.

Bouges currently belongs to M. and Mme. Viquier, who
maintain it beautifully.

131

CHÂTEAU DES GROTTEAUX, NEAR CHAMBORD

The Château des Grotteaux at Huisson-sur-Cosson, lies near the village of Chiteau across the Loire from Blois. Dating from the early seventeenth century, it is remarkably similar in plan and design to the earlier Manor of Vonne. It is reasonable to assume that Vonne served as a model for this château.

Constructed primarily as a retreat for the sage Guillaume de Ribier, it is replete with engraved inscriptions and sentences in Latin.

Particularly impressive is the carved marble fireplace in the drawing room. Note the inscription in Latin on the beams which support the ceiling.

The porcelain stove is said to have come from the nearby château of Chambord after the death of the Maréchal de Saxe. The present owner is Monsieur B. Renauld.

134

FRANCE

BAGATELLE
AT ABBEVILLE

A country house, Bagatelle at Abbeville was built in three stages between 1751 and 1793. Originally, it was simply a one-story building with a terrace; an attic story was added in 1763. In fact, this addition is a wonder to architects to this very day, as it in no way detracts from the symmetry or coherence of the pavilion, but rather enhances it dramatically. A slated-roof story was added in 1793.

The house was commissioned by Abraham van Robais, a rich merchant who was the first manufacturer of fine clothes in Abbeville and all of the North of France.

The interior, although small in scale, is pure Louis XV style of great beauty. The first floor includes a summer salon, which connects to a winter salon and to a dining room—a simple plan adopted by the merchant in order to receive his clients. The fireplace in the winter salon is of ornately carved wood and together with the wooden moldings and paneling is painted blue. A touch of Louis XVI is evident in the Pompeian arabesques painted on the panels in the summer salon during the latter part of the eighteenth century.

Bagatelle is an enchanting house, kept in superb condition. Its present owner is the distinguished architect M. J. de Wailly.

138

BEAUMONT-
SUR-VINGEANNE

The very elegant and diminutive
residence of Beaumont-sur-Vingeanne appears to be a "folie"
located on the Île Saint-Louis in Paris which has
wandered off to the country.

Built by the Abbé Joly di Richebourg, a member of the court of Louis
XV, around 1750, the one-story front facade is approached
by a double staircase, and is dominated by a pedimented entrance
door. Above the pediment is a clock and a weathervane. The
four front windows are topped with keystones, and a balustrade with
light vases and figurines crowns the elevation.

In the rear, facing the garden, a basement story, which contains the
dining room and kitchen, supports a balustraded terrace,
which descends to the ground in a double staircase. The center of the
facade is enhanced by three arched French doors, and the
interiors have fine boiseries, and one salon includes
panels by Hubert Robert.

It is a charming and very sophisticated house. The Abbé must have
been, like so many of his time, very much a man of the
world.

Beaumont-sur-Vingeanne is currently owned by the Marquise
de Montmort. Her son, the Count Louis de Montmort, shares the
house with her.

143

LA BECHELLERIE, NEAR TOURS

La Bechellerie is a charming little house near Tours in Touraine. It was the final home of Anatole France, who in 1914 sought refuge there from the approaching Germans. This small retreat will always be associated with his name.

The house was built toward the end of the sixteenth century by M. Beschel. In the courtyard stands a marble statue of a nude woman, which originally came from the garden of Madame Elizabeth, the guillotined sister of Louis XVI. The unpretentious pavilion has all the charms that one finds in the simple, beautiful houses of the French countryside.

SPAIN

CASITA DE ARRIBA AT EL ESCORIAL
CASITA DE PRINCIPE AT EL ESCORIAL
CASITA DE PRINCIPE AT EL PRADO

THE CASITA DE ARRIBA AT EL ESCORIAL

Perhaps out of sibling rivalry, the
Infante Don Gabriel de Bourbon, younger brother of the
Crown Prince, also commissioned Don Juan de Villanueva to construct
a little house for him. The Casita de Arriba, built around
1772, is two stories high with a subdued, harmonious facade. The
court is surrounded by Ionic columns with a pool in front
of the facade.

This granite pavilion affords a beautiful view of the valley,
but doesn't quite hold a candle to the Don Carlos amusement casino
in appointments. The interior includes delicate ceiling
paintings, beautifully upholstered furniture and impressive cut-glass
and bronze chandeliers, originally in the Casita de Principe.

THE CASITA DE PRINCIPE AT EL ESCORIAL

In 1772, Crown Prince Don Carlos, who later became Charles IV of Spain, commissioned the architect Don Juan de Villanueva to build him a little house, or casino, for amusement on the eastern side of the San Lorenzo Monastery. The facade of this gray granite pavilion features a portico supported by four elegant Tuscan columns.

Since the young prince was an avid collector of beautiful things, he filled the pavilion with exquisite furniture, clocks, tapestries, chandeliers and an impressive collection of two hundred and twenty-six porcelains of British Wedgwood. Ceiling paintings are in the Pompeian style with the floors in polychrome and black and white marble and jasper. Perhaps the most beautiful are the floors of "fine woods," inlaid to form foliage, flowers, and urns.

The dining room, the largest in the house, is the most luxurious, with hangings and chairs in green satin and a Spanish Empire mahogany-and-marble-mosaic dining table supported by sixteen Corinthian columns with gilded bronze capitals. Overhead the great forty-eight-light chandelier in cut-glass and gilded bronze completes the décor.

On the grounds are redwood trees sent by Spaniards from California when they occupied it.

CASITA DE PRINCIPE
AT EL PRADO

Built in 1772 by the architect Lopez Corona, the Casita de Principe owes its existence to Princess Maria Luisa of Parma's desire to have a place of retirement where she could gather with her intimates far away from the rigorous palace etiquette.

Simply constructed, the one-floor brick and stone building's facade is a portico with two Ionic columns. The groundfloor is rectangular in form with eight rooms and one circular hallway, which overlooks part of the garden. The beauty of the entrance approach has been injured by the highway cutting close by. The interior is magnificently decorated, with the hall done in splendid marbles and with doors and windows overlooking the garden.

The Stucco Room, so-called because of the quantity and beauty of stucco imitating marble is neoclassic in style. Another room, the Velvet Room, is so-called because the tapestry and furniture upholstery is of velvet printed with flowers on an ochre background.

Paintings of various Spanish artists as well as of Lorenzo Tiepolo and Raphael Mengs are hung throughout the house.

SPAIN

ENGLAND

THE BOAT PAVILION
AT SYON HOUSE

The pavilion at Syon is really an embellished boat house. It was originally built at the end of the eighteenth century by the second Duke of Northumberland from designs by architect Robert Mylne. Built as a surprise present for the Duke's wife, it was used by her and her lady friends as a place to take tea before going boating in the Thames.

The present pavilion was built over a Tudor boathouse which stood on the spot for many years. Recent excavations have revealed even older wooden pillars dating from Caesar's conquest of Britain. It is assumed that the Roman crossed the river at this point before the first battle of Brentford. Lady Jane Grey also sailed from Syon to her imprisonment in the Tower of London.

The original plan has been changed extensively in recent years, but all in keeping with the original architecture and interior design. The house has been superbly modernized by the present owner, Mrs. Diana Daly.

ENGLAND

CHISWICK VILLA

Work on Chiswick Villa was begun in 1725, under the Third Earl of Burlington, and completed shortly after 1729, according to dates carved on the fireplace in the Red Velvet Room. Modeled after the Villa Capra by Palladio near Vicenza, it also shows the influence of Scamozzi.

Lord Burlington was an ardent devotee of the Palladian style, having acquired many drawings of Italian buildings by Palladio and his pupils. At Chiswick he drew substantially from the Italian's designs; he was not, however, merely a copyist. He maintained an adherence to the Roman style, but also incorporated his own ideas.

Palladio's four matching porticos at the Villa Capra are replaced by two grand staircases, at the entrance and garden fronts. The Italian's rather squat circular dome is replaced by an octagonal one with large semicircular windows providing the extra light necessitated by the English climate. The central hall, an octagon, provides space for profuse decoration. On the garden front, Palladio's four-square plan is replaced by a large gallery with open archways at either end.

The interior décor is presumably by William Kent, whose designs, particularly of the fireplaces, are taken from Inigo Jones.

THE STOKE PARK PAVILIONS

At Stoke Park in Towcaster, there are two charming pavilions built in 1630 by Inigo Jones. The two curving colonnades originally were joined to a main house which no longer stands.

Behind the pavilions at a nonobtrusive distance stands a house built much later in the architecture of an earlier period.

The garden below the pavilions has water pieces which look out over the countryside. The pavilions belong today to R. D. Chancellor, Esq. and A. Revai, Esq.

164

THE BRIGHTON PAVILION

Right smack there in the middle of the
Regency community of Brighton is the seaside pleasure
palace of King George IV. This is no ordinary palace, and is in effect,
perhaps the most foolish of all the "folies" on earth. A little
bit of old India and China, right there only an hour's ride from
London. Complete with minarets, onion domes, tracery, and
every bit of foo-foo inspired by either the fantastic whimsy of high
camp or simple deranged madness, Brighton stands as the
monument to the extreme romanticism of the early
nineteenth century.

The interior, perhaps a decorator's Vatican, contains Chinese
Chippendale, bamboo dados, dolphin furniture,
sleigh-shaped settees, nubian figures, and every conceivable kind of
plant and animal life furniture.

The dining room may well have served as a model for the now defunct
Roxy Theater. High up on the domed ceiling is a painting of
tanna leaves. Beneath that an immense chandelier, which "contains" a
dragon with fire coming from his mouth, stained glass, six
large tulip-shaped flowers from which hang six more dragons.

It is actually . . . not to be believed, but yet, somehow quite
beautiful.

169

WORCESTER LODGE
AT BADMINTON

Badminton, the home of the Dukes of
Beaufort, has always, as has the family, been famous for
hunting. It was the third Duke, who came into the title in 1714, who
had William Kent, the fashionable architect of the day,
transform the house into what is essentially the existing one, and
expand the spacious grounds and the radiating avenues for
the pleasure of the hunt.

A mile from the house and on an axis to it, the third Duke,
with Kent as his architect, built the gate lodge known as Worcester. It
has a noble room on its second floor from which one could
follow the hunt without participating.

STOURHEAD, WILTON

The famous gardens at Stourhead have
many temples and pavilions, two of which are shown here.

The Temple of the Sun stands on a rise above a lake of fourteen acres
formed by the order of Sir Richard Colt Hoare in 1822. It is
a lovely circular temple with two statues by Cheere in its colonnade.
The name Temple of the Sun derives from that at Baalbec,
from which this is copied.

THE GOTHIC PAVILION AT FRAMPTON-ON-SEVERN

The garden at Frampton-on-Severn includes a canal which terminates in a Gothic pavilion consisting of two octagons with an octagonal turret at the back containing a staircase. The doors and windows all have ogee profiles and the sashes hexagonal frames.

The pavilion is sturdily built, containing fireplaces and impressive cornices. The designer may have been William Halfpenny, who probably completed the pavilion after the main house was erected.

Frampton Court and the Gothic Pavilion are the property of Mr. and Mrs. Clifford, descendants of the original Lord of the Manor, who are most gracious about showing the houses.

IRELAND

MARINO CASINO
DRAMOLAND LOOKOUT
HUNTING LODGE FOLIE, LIMERIC

MARINO CASINO

The Marino Casino, an Irish National Monument, built for the Lord Viscount who later became Earl of Charlemont, is a classic jewel set among ever-increasing banalities. It was designed in London by Sir William Chambers. The plans and elevations for it were first published in his *Treatise on Civil Architecture* (1739). Simon Verpyle, a Dublin dealer, constructed it between 1767 and 1771.

The white Portland stone pavilion is set on a pedestal, with crouching lions at each corner, enclosed by free-standing Doric columns that support an entablature with pediments and balustrades. Two sculptured vases serve as chimneys at each end of the roof.

Three sides of the house are surrounded by a well, which gives light and access to the kitchen, scullery, and utility rooms. The fourth side is distinguished by a facade-length flight of steps.

Lord Charlemont, one of the worldly Irishmen of his period and a patron of Piranesi, used the design of Chambers, which originally had been rendered for an end pavilion at Harewood House. The Casino once had a splendid view of Dublin Bay, but now one looks out on the rather sordid, quasi-Gothic O'Brien Institute.

The interior is beautifully decorated and is now, after years of neglect, being restored by the National Monuments Division of Ireland.

DRAMOLAND LOOKOUT

Little is known of the Dramoland Lookout, which stands on a gentle hillside, below which the hunt went by.

It is presumed that it was built in the eighteenth century for the ladies and those gentlemen who from age or girth could not join in, but enjoyed watching their friends ride by.

HUNTING LODGE FOLIE, LIMERIC

Another surprising "folie" that raises the
hackles of one's imagination is not far from Limeric. Here,
on a hillock with a superb view over the hunting country below, is a
small tower, the main room of which is one story up. To
reach it you must mount an imposing series of steps.
Its background is unrecorded, but surely it was built by a
hulky sire, too heavy to follow the hound, but too loving to miss it. So
here on his magnificent horse, he could ride up to watch the
hunt.

Friends would join him for drinks and food, which were
prepared in the room below.

Today, a contented cow chews its cud and blocks the
entrance to the curious.